Extreme
wealth
should be taxed

J.P. Fonteijn

©2023 Jean-Paul Fonteijn

First printing: February 2023
Publisher: SRT Publishing
Editorial: Haags Bureau | Boekenmakers
Design cover and interior: Haags Bureau | Boekenmakers
Illustration front cover: Bigfish animation

www.superrichtax.com

ISBN: 978-90-833147-2-3 (print)
        978-90-833147-3-0 (eBook)
NUR: 903

I hope you enjoy reading and I hope I can inspire you to vote for this manifesto. Let us all unite so that we can turn the world in the right direction again. With the Super Rich Tax, it's possible!

Jean-Paul Fonteijn

Contents

Foreword

There is something terrible wrong with the world today. Inequality and environmental degradation continue to increase, and our gut feeling is that things will not go the right way if we continue in the way we do now. Revolutionary changes must be set in motion, otherwise there will be hard times ahead for an increasing portion of humanity.

Economic inequality has created five different types of people, all of whom perceive and experience today's world in their own way. To properly explain this, and the disastrous consequences of 'extreme wealth', I will address each type in different chapters: The Underprivileged, The Privileged, The Rich, The Extreme Rich and The Exorbitantly Rich. The goal is to provide a better future for a large part of humanity, our children and their children.

First the good news: if we act quickly, we can still save humanity!

'For a long time we thought the earth was flat, but then we discovered that the earth was round.'

'For a very long time we thought 'extreme wealth' was normal, but then we discovered that we should tax the 'extreme rich."

Chapter 1

The Super Rich Tax, And A Short Introduction

Extreme wealth should be taxed

By means of this book, I aim to make as many people as possible aware of the facts below:

---

1 There is an extremely destructive concentration of wealth in the modern world.

---

2 This extreme concentration of wealth is the core problem of a lot of other major issues on our planet.

---

3 As a result of this extreme concentration of wealth, more and more underprivileged people are leading unhappy lives.

4 This extreme concentration of wealth creates an extremely dangerous accumulation of financial power among a small group of rich people.

5 The extreme concentration of wealth is making our economies increasingly unhealthy.

6 It is making our governments poorer and poorer.

7 It is making it increasingly likely that our children and grandchildren will be disadvantaged, and will lead unhappy lives.

8 Fortunately, there is also good news: we can stop the current concentration of extreme wealth by introducing a Super Rich Tax. In this way, we can move the planet in the right direction again. The exact details about the Super Rich Tax will be described later in this chapter.

I hear you thinking: what kind of book is this?

This will be answered too, I promise you. First I would like to introduce myself. I am 53, live in Driebergen in The Netherlands and earn my living as a freelance project manager. You may now be wondering: what does this have to do with the extraordinary propositions in this book?

Nothing at all, except that I want to take you into the personal background of the author of this book. I am someone without noteworthy status. In today's world it is common for the majority to listen to people who do have a noteworthy status; people who have achieved something exceptional in life. For example, a politician who lots of people voted for, or someone who has had a successful business career, but also famous athletes or movie stars or, in other words, people who have lots of money. There are also plenty of other reasons why someone gains a noteworthy status in the eyes of people. As stated before, I am not someone with a noteworthy status. Perhaps you'll now close this book, because after all, why read a book by a man without standing, and who has such grandiose propositions?

I'll make an effort regardless. Many people have figured out by now that the world is squeaking and creaking, and humanity is suffering as a result. There are climate and environmental problems, wars and refugee flows and poverty on a broad scale. Various economies must be kept alive with all kinds of emergency bandages. Most people sense that it is time for a revolutionary change, because otherwise an increasing portion of humanity will have an even harder time.

Indeed, a revolution. A revolution, you say? Yes, but first: what can we actually deduce from previous revolutions, such as, for example, the French Revolution?

The French Revolution was a revolt by French workers and peasants that took place between 1789 and 1799. It brought about an unprecedented upheaval of power, which until then had been in the hands of the French king and nobility. The people felt that they were oppressed. Not to mention, people were regularly starving. There was bread, plenty of it even, but it was unaffordable: it was way too expensive. The 'grey', or 'common man', rebelled against poverty, class struggle and government incompetence. The symbolic starting point of the revolution was the storming of the Bastille, a prison in Paris. On 14 July, a day still commemorated in France, the people freed the seven men imprisoned there. Earlier that day they had already looted the weapons depot of the Hôtel des Invalides, where guns and muskets were stored. After the storming, much changed in France. The former king and his consort were tried by a tribunal and sentenced to death. France became a republic in which citizens were given more power.

The French Revolution is considered one of the most successful uprisings in the history of our planet, and as the beginning of far-reaching and lasting changes throughout Europe."

People with status are often people who succeed because they conform (often unconsciously) to the current frameworks that 'the world' applies. During a revolution, however, something outside of these frameworks must happen. Revolutionary change therefore rarely, if ever, comes from people with significant status. The past teaches us that revolutionary change arises primarily from within the people. Consider the people who initiated the French Revolution, as well as the many other revolutions that were initiated by ordinary people who believed in something. For example, in Portugal, Tunisia, Egypt and Cuba.

Now you may say: 'Well explained and all, but why should I read this book? There have probably been hundreds of thousands of people with similar ideas, so should I read all of their books too? No? So why should I read yours?'

Okay, you have a point. However, I will do my best to captivate you for as long as possible and take you along with me in my knowledge and experiences and the resulting ideas. In short, I am trying to make the world's population, some 8 billion people, aware of the importance of a Super Rich Tax. Indeed, pretty ambitious...

But before I get into things, I'd like to tell a bit more about myself. I experienced a happy childhood. I had been thinking a lot about global inequality all my life. From a somewhat shy boy, I slowly became someone who was more opinionated, who acted according to Sartre's prudence:

> *'I don't look down on anyone except people who look down on others.'*

Throughout my student years, I encountered a quote that was very inspiring to me. It turned out to be a quote by Swiss philosopher Henri-Frédéric Amiel (1821-1881):

> *'Reality spoils, if the ideal does not add its salt to it. But the ideal itself becomes a poison if it does not connect with reality.'*

I was particularly impressed by this quote, especially because I noticed that a lot of idealism in the world didn't work out that well in practice. My challenge was to identify those ideals that could lead to positive results. But how do you find out whether an ideal is effective in practice or not? And how do you find out that the ideal is going to act as 'salt', and not 'poison'?

Let's look at an example. The following ideal is especially popular these days:

> *'Because of the current environmental and inequality problems, we need to drastically transform the current economy.'*

One pitfall of humanity is that it often reaches too far to find a solution. Unfortunately, the ideal then becomes poison.

Current economies are about 90% fine, they just need to become more circular, and the Super Rich Tax should be introduced. Two concrete areas for improvement, then, and nothing more.

Indeed, we don't have to turn the entire economic system upside down or burn down the entire current economic model. This is counterproductive and will only lead to more misery, or in other words: the ideal becomes poison. Despite all the problems we face today, we will also have to recognise the positive parts of the current economic models.

After my student years, I continued to keep wondering what really was the root cause of all the world's problems. From this point on, I enjoyed delving into Charles Darwin's theory of evolution, Yuval Noah Harari's history book Sapiens and Thomas Piketty's YouTube videos on economics.

I consciously developed into a generalist in terms of my thinking, because I did not want to limit myself to a particular expertise. I sensed that complex world problems consist of multiple areas of expertise, and can never be solved from one single area of expertise. In the Netherlands we often say 'to measure is to know'. But unfortunately we cannot solve today's complex problems on this basis. Within specific fields, the 'to measure is to know' approach can be successful, of course, but when you start to broaden those measurements and apply them outside your field, it may lead to wrong and even dangerous conclusions. Every specialist tends to have tunnel vision, and by focusing too much on details, this creates the pitfall that the expert or specialist sometimes fails to see the bigger picture.

The mass psychologist and communication scientist Jaap van Ginneken (1943-present) therefore states that subject specialists should take second place in solving world problems. After all, to understand and solve complex issues, you require broad generalist-thinkers who understand the complexity of the world around them.

In my working life, I was able to make good money as a project manager, drawing on my accumulated reserves with moral ambitions to go into business. From there, I came into contact with the world of investors and the wealthy, which gave me many insights. From this combination of theoretical and practical knowledge, I figured out why humanity is facing so many different problems, especially in terms of poverty and environmental problems.

Okay, now that you know who I am, let's get back to the core problem at play in our world today: extreme wealth concentration.

How are we so sure that extreme wealth concentration exists in the world?

Below is some evidence for this extreme wealth concentration:

1 Professor Thomas Piketty's books and his figures in the World Inequality Database (WID).

2 Professor Jan Tobochnik's mathematical model, where if you just keep calculating long enough you'll see that in the end there will remain one person who is in the possession of all the wealth in the world. Take a look at the video on www.superrichtax.com.

3 The presence of extremely wealthy people on our earth, who own wealth up to even 200 billion dollars.

4 The presence of extremely many underprivileged people in our world.

5 Due to the painful visibility of wealth concentration following the COVID-19 pandemic, in which a great many more people than before have fallen through the poverty line, while at the same time a record number of luxury vehicles were sold.

Beyond this evidence, it is also amazingly simple to reason out how the current concentration of wealth has come about. I will explain why a fair economy can never exist with extreme differences in wealth.

In a healthy, fair economy, everyone pays a certain amount for a product they enjoy, and each person decides to what maximum they go in purchasing this product.
Someone who is extremely wealthy who wishes to buy a certain product knows that most people who desire that same product are much poorer than him. Therefore, this wealthy person can quietly wait for the time when everyone who is less wealthy than him has been negotiated out of the product on sale.
The extremely rich person can simply wait until he knows the price that the poorer people have arrived at among themselves. Once everyone has finished negotiation, the extremely rich person arrives. With a poker face, he offers 1 euro more than the amount the poorer people agreed to by negotiation.
And, pay attention now: the extremely rich person buys the product for much less money than he was willing to spend on it before!

He had much more money to spare, but there was no need at all to stretch his credit card beyond the relatively low amount the poorer people had determined among themselves.

Professor Jan Tobochnik's mathematical models show that based on this principle, there is a wealth concentration going on where, if you keep calculating long enough, eventually there will remain one person who owns all the money in the whole world.

Being rich, or having more assets than others, simply gives you a better bargaining position for economic transactions. This means the current extreme concentration of wealth is surprisingly simple to explain. The above example also shows that with the current extreme wealth differences between the poor and extremely rich, there is no case of fair trade.

Current economies no longer work fairly and are therefore extremely unhealthy.

Roughly speaking, the world at present consists largely of
• people with few possessions (the non-rich) and
• people with a lot of possessions (the rich).

People with few possessions (the non-rich) are people who:

---

1 Earn money by working, or who are entitled to benefits.

---

2 Spend money as a medium of exchange in the economy.

---

3 Spend money as a tax payment to the government.

---

4 Spend money as pension contributions for their retirement.

People with a lot of possessions (the rich) are people who:

---

1 Don't have to work (some do, but they don't have to do this to earn a living, they already earn a lot with their assets).

---

2 Make a lot of money through their assets.

---

3 Spend their income from assets to purchase even more assets.

---

4 Spend relatively little money as a medium of exchange in the economy and relatively little money as tax payments to the government.

Therefore, within the world's current legislations, money flows at the country and global level from 'the people with few possessions' (the non-rich) to 'the people with many possessions (the rich)'.

Furthermore, the number of wealthy people with extremely large amounts of property is getting smaller and smaller.

At the same time, the people who remain in the small group of exorbitantly wealthy are getting richer and richer per person. This process of money flowing to an ever smaller group of exorbitantly wealthy people (the process of wealth concentration) was substantiated with figures a decade ago in the books of world-renowned French economist Thomas Piketty. After the publication of his first book, his ideas and figures received worldwide attention.

All the way into politics, Piketty was invited to come speak and explain his theory and plans, but the wealth concentration problem that everyone focused on at the time, has actually been slowly disappearing from the world's agenda.

When the pandemic broke out in 2020, peaking in 2022, it turned out to have not only caused wealth concentration among the rich to become even more extreme, but also that this concentration had become incredibly visible.

After the peak of the pandemic, lots of people were found to have fallen through the poverty line, and poor people who were already at the bottom became even poorer. At the same time, however, never before had so many luxury cars been sold!

Ergo: those with few possessions have become much poorer, and those with many possessions have become much richer.

Extreme inequality, and thus the extreme concentration of wealth among the rich, is currently – we are talking February 2023 – gaining media attention again, but the danger in doing so is that the topic will soon slowly disappear once more.

So we must grab this current opportunity to do something about wealth concentration!

Why must we do something about the current extreme concentration of wealth?

Because this concentration of wealth has two very negative effects on the world:

---

1 The first effect is that the small group that holds almost all of the world's property and/or wealth is becoming smaller and smaller. This means the people in that little group are becoming much richer per individual than they were before. The American business magazine Forbes produces a list of annual billionaires, as well as a list of the 400 richest people in the United States. The latest official figures are from 2018 and those put Jeff Bezos of Amazon at number one. At the time he had assets worth 112 billion dollars. Bill Gates of Microsoft had assets of 90 billion dollars and Warren Buffet of Berhshire Hatahway accounted for assets of 84 billion dollars. Many other lists are also published annually, such as in the Netherlands the 'Quote 500' by Quote magazine, which too attracts great attention. Wealth concentration among only a handful of people in the world, while the rest of the people are getting poorer, leads to a dangerous concentration of financial power among the small group of exorbitantly rich.

---

2 The second effect is, due to the current concentration of wealth, more and more money is flowing away from the group of people with few possessions, while they serve as the very basis of financing our economies and governments.

In Chapter 2, I will explain how wealth concentration is making our economies increasingly unhealthy and our governments increasingly poorer.

So...

To summarise. Wealth concentration causes the total wealth of those with few possessions to get smaller and smaller, but because these people form the basis of our economies, these economies become financially unhealthier. This has resulted in our economies to have to be saved by all types of artificial means. Keeping interest rates artificially low and additional money printing are perfect examples of such interventions. Only this way, with much squeaking and creaking, can our economies be kept running. But for how long exactly?

The good news

And now for the good news: we can make our creaking economies and governments healthy again if we reduce the extreme wealth concentration and extreme inequality on our planet in a revolutionary way. If we start doing that now, economies and governments will become healthy again, so there will be more budget available to structurally solve many other current problems.

How should we approach this?
Below I explain how we can use the Super Rich Tax to address the current disastrous concentration of wealth.

---

1   We can address the dangerous concentration of financial wealth among a small group of exorbitantly wealthy people by means of the Super Rich Tax: this means taxing wealth above 10 million euros at 30% or more.

Because most entrepreneurs and shareholders prefer not to pay taxes on their assets, they will try to stay under 10 million euros in assets.

Therefore, they will start transferring their shares in parts, for example to the top people within their organisation. This is positive because then the enormous wealth no longer remains with one rich person, but is distributed among several people. Whether the amount should be exactly 10 million euros or not, we will need to investigate further. It may be wise to have a transition period and subsequently move to a higher amount.

---

2 To make our economies and governments healthy again, we need to make sure money flows back to the people with few possessions. We can do this by means of the Super Rich Tax. By setting the guideline that if a company has a positive balance sheet and makes a profit – let's say 3 million euros, for convenience – then at least 50% of that 3 million euros of profit must be divided equally among all employees of that company. The remaining 50% may remain in the company as equity or be distributed as dividends to shareholders. That way, employees share in the profits, and it becomes much more transparent what amounts remain on the shareholders' coattails.

Whether the amount should be exactly 50% of 3 million euros, we shall need to investigate further. It may be wise to have a transitional phase and start with a lower percentage.

And now a warning!

Meanwhile, there are noises from some wealthy people indicating that they are willing to pay a little wealth tax, but their proposals do not go nearly far enough.

In fact, their suggestions may even be dangerous, because they may throw sand in the eyes of those with few possessions. These proposals of a few well-meaning super-rich people do not go nearly far enough. They come up with proposals for paying 2% to 5% wealth tax. These percentages are not going to stop the ever-increasing, world-destroying concentration of wealth. In Chapter 2, I explain why these rates are not enough and only have a dampening effect on the growth of wealth concentration. Or in other words: wealth concentration will continue to increase, but only slightly less harshly, while unfortunately just as destructively. So the danger is that these friendly proposals from the super-rich themselves will only lull those with few assets to sleep.

This book is a call for all people to wake up.
We can't let the super-rich blind us when they kindly suggest a tiny bit of wealth tax. Never mind that we should praise the super-rich who come up with these proposals, they really have good intentions after all!

There needs to be a fair bit of pressure 'from below', with which the ordinary people clearly indicate that it is really high time for a new narrative. Without pressure from below, those good intentions of the super-rich to pay a little tax are not going to get us anywhere at all. The super-rich simply operate within the frameworks of today's world, and then you will arrive at only 2% to 5% indeed. But things really need to be different! With that 2% to 5%, you will keep the common people happy for a short time, while inequality just keeps growing.

There will really have to be much more pressure to put a ceiling on individual's wealth and redistribute money worldwide. The pressure will have to come from ordinary people, after which politicians can take over. That's the only way revolutionary changes will come about; remember the French Revolution I mentioned before? Now is exactly the time! The time to make ordinary people aware that they are poor because the rich are so wealthy!

Our unhealthy economies, bankrupt governments, extreme inequalities and the gigantic climate problems can only be solved if we start bringing about a revolutionary change, with the introduction of the Super Rich Tax.

Chapter 2

How our economies and governments went bankrupt

Stop the extreme concentration of wealth with the Super Rich Tax

About four thousand years ago, there was no such thing as 'property' and 'returns'; money was made by simply working for it. To clarify what the world was like then, I'd like to tell a little story of a society that existed back then.

That society consists of four villages. People from those four villages go to the market every evening and sell their products to each other. Four families live in each of the four villages, all consisting of a married couple with children, and one of the two parents is at work every day. In the first family, one of the parents goes to fetch ten gallons of water every day from a lake down the road, a parent of the second family picks fifty bananas every day, a parent of the third family chops five blocks of wood from the forest every day, and a parent of the fourth family catches five rabbits every day.

All four of these people leave early in the morning, and all four return around the same time every evening. They then visit the market together and sell their day's produce.

Suppose euros existed in this village (including surrounding villages), and suppose they agreed among themselves that one day's work equals 50 euros, then they could calculate as follows.

> 1 litre of water is worth 5 euros
> 1 banana is worth 1 euro
> 1 block of wood is worth 10 euros
> 1 rabbit is also worth 10 euros
>
> Or in other words:
> for 1 block of wood you can get 2 litres of water, 10 bananas or 1 rabbit

Back to our village for a moment: so every evening our four people visit the central market where they meet people from other villages. Everyone sells products to each other.

Our four people manage to sell all the products they have acquired that day, earning all four of them 50 euros. They can make a good living from this money. The four families each have a nice house and live in good harmony with each other and the people from the other villages.

To make clear what effect 'possession' can have on an economy, I will now depict it in our little example society. Here we go:

The village has recently seen the following events take place: the parents of one of the four families appeared to have been a bit more frugal and also a bit more cunning than the parents in the other families in recent years. This couple had saved some money in recent years. As a result, at one point these people managed to buy the forest, banana tree and lake. It all became their property.

The new owners agreed with the three other families that they could still fetch water, pick bananas and cut wood, but that they would have to give 90% of their yields to the owners. Since the three other families had no other work, and since there were families from other villages lurking to take over their work if they stopped, they were more or less forced to agree to the condition. The daily income of the three families was suddenly reduced to just 5 euros per day. And the fourth family, now the owner of everything, suddenly, without doing anything for it, had a substantially higher daily income. By the way, the fourth family also continued catching rabbits, so they now had a total of 3 times 45 plus 50 = 185 euros per day in income.

The three other families, with their meagre incomes of 5 euros a day, could only just about make ends meet, and in one blow had become underprivileged, because they had opportunity to accumulate savings to buy property of their own in the future. There was no way they could still save up the necessary start-up capital. The houses of the three low-income families were also increasingly poorly maintained due to the lack of money and even began to fall into disrepair. In addition, the three families had many worries, because they had to calculate and budget every day to make ends meet.

The richer family that had lived so frugally had become rich so quickly, that the family had now moved into a very large house. There the family members lived in opulence, and meanwhile their wealth grew day by day, without the family having to do anything. Soon they had far more money than they could spend. They were looking for new property, because they had to do something with all that money. They were looking for land to purchase, which would make them even richer in the future. This allowed them to buy an even bigger house, and even more land... and so on and so on...

The above two examples demonstrate four negative effects of extreme ownership and extreme wealth:

---

1 That someone with extreme possession makes much more money than someone without possession or with very little possession.

---

2 That money flows from those with no or little property to those with more, or a lot of property. People with more or many possessions earn the most money, following which they can purchase even more possessions.

---

3 Asset concentration makes the economy unhealthier, as the total amount of free money on the global market used as a medium of exchange (the actual economy) becomes much less.

---

4 The concentration of wealth makes the government poorer and ultimately bankrupt, because the total amount of money received from payroll taxes paid by disadvantaged people is getting lower and lower. After all, in all current economies, governments receive their money primarily from payroll taxes, and virtually none from capital income.

I am now going to explain a bit more about the negative effects of points 3 and 4. First I will explain the negative effects of point 3, about the increasingly unhealthier economies.

In the village, a total of 4 x 50 euros = 200 euros was used at the start as a means of exchange.
However, after one of the families acquires land, 3 x 5 euros = 15 euros is used as a means of exchange. After all, the three propertyless families together now have only 15 euros to spend per day.
The fourth family, having acquired property, suddenly earns 185 euros a day.

The question now is: how many euros of these 185 euros will this family use as a means of exchange?

Indeed, this will never be the full 185 euros. Before this family owned property, they used 50 euros a day as a means of exchange, and since they are a little richer now, chances are that they will spend a little more money a day. However, they will definitely not suddenly start spending 185 euros a day.

It is more likely that their spending pattern grows from 50 euros to 70 euros.

So what will happen now?

The total amount of money used as a means of exchange has become (15 euros + 70 euros) = 85 euros.

The total amount of money used as a means of exchange determines the actual economy. First the daily actual economy in the village was 200 euros, however later, when one of the four families acquired property, it became less!

The mathematical example makes it clear that because of the wealth of one of the families, the total size of the actual economy fell by 115 euros to 85 euros. So that's considerably less than 200 euros.

This demonstrates that because of the concentration of wealth (money owned by a small group of rich people but which isn't actively used), our economies become unhealthier.

Many people believe extremely rich people use all their wealth to invest, which in turn benefits the economy, but unfortunately in practice it turns out that far too often their wealth is used to buy back shares of a company, and to take over other companies and merge, after which many employees are forced to be laid off. This, unfortunately, is the opposite of healthy economic development.

For more details, please refer to Professor Peter Ricchiuti's video on www.superrichtax.com.

Now to the explanation of the negative effect of point 4: increasingly poorer governments.

Because in our current world we always tax wages much higher (payroll tax) than income from property and assets (capital income tax), in the following example I will apply a 50% payroll tax and a 10% capital income tax. At the start, our village levies payroll tax on the total salary of 200 euros. After one of the four families acquires property, the total amount of wages drops to 3 x 5 euros and 1 x 50 euros = a total of 65 euros.

Now suppose the payroll tax is 50%, then the government of a village with four working families receives 200 euros x 50% = 100 euros of tax per day in payroll taxes.

But in the situation where one of the four families has acquired property and only three families are still working, the government receives only 65 euros x 50% = 32.50 euros per day.

The capital income tax is 10%, so with four working families from the village, the government levies 0 euros per day. After all, none of the four families owns capital, property or assets.

In the new situation, where one of the four families owns property, the government levies (3 x 45 x 10%) = 13.50 euros per day in capital income tax.

So in the first example, the government receives 100 (100 + 0) euros per day in taxes, and in the second example, the government receives 46 (32.50 + 13.50) euros per day in taxes.

These the calculations show that the concentration of one family's wealth (thanks to property, capital or assets) not only makes our economies unhealthier, but also makes our governments poorer.

In most countries (including the Netherlands), wages of people who work are taxed much more than income from capital (or property, and wealth), while the owners of capital who pay little tax do not even have to work.

The Central Planning Bureau (CPB) in the Netherlands indicated on 25 March, 2022 that:

> 'Rich people pay much less tax than other households. The income of the very richest households consists largely of capital income such as interest, dividends, rents and corporate profits. These are taxed much less than wage income', the researchers said.

The governments of other countries, too, receive much more tax revenue from payroll taxes – that is, through taxing working people - than from taxing capital income of rich people.

It's also good to realise that we haven't even yet factored in another huge positive effect of the Super Rich Tax: if economies become fair and healthy again, many more people will feel empowered and happy. This means more positive and innovative energy will be released in the world, which will give us, including our economies and governments, a further boost.

The people who pay payroll taxes and have no or few assets are ultimately the basis for healthy economies and governments. Since all the money of these ordinary people is now flowing away to the rich, it is not surprising that the economies and governments of this world are becoming increasingly unhealthy.

> *'In the end, we are not going to survive this way as humanity, because the more unhealthy our economies and governments, the greater the likelihood of unrest and new wars.'*

Please note

Around the time this book went to press, Oxfam Novib started the petition 'Tax the Super Rich'. In itself, it is good that this issue is starting to be talked about more, but unfortunately Oxfam Novib is only talking about taxing 'income earned from assets', or in other words 'capital income'. This will indeed make governments richer, but unfortunately it only has a dampening effect on the growth of wealth concentration.

So in effect one is taxing the growth of wealth, but not the wealth itself. After all, assets will continue to grow, they will just grow a little slower. Because the asset concentration is not addressed, our unhealthy economies will still increasingly become even more unhealthy, and that is precisely the heart of the problem we want to address.

Oxfam Novib is calling on governments worldwide to initiate the measures below.

---

1 Oxfam Novib states: introduce a mix of taxes that ensures that the richest 1% of people must pay at least 60% of their income in taxes.

---

2 Oxfam Novib states: introduce a one-time solidarity tax and tax on excessive profits by companies profiting from global crises.

---

3 Oxfam Novib states: use tax revenues to fight inequality, for example by investing in health care and education, food security and a fair and sustainable economy.

Unfortunately, these measures by Oxfam Novib do not go far enough, because they are only talking about 60% of the income of a super-rich person. If we tax the income of a super-rich person, the government will get a little richer, but unfortunately this has no effect whatsoever on our unhealthy economies because it does not address asset concentration. At best, it dampens a bit the growth of wealth concentration. Just like the initiatives suggested by the super-rich themselves, Oxfam Novib has (probably unwittingly and well-intentioned) set in motion something that could backfire. As with the well-intentioned initiatives of the super-rich themselves, they may lull us back to sleep until we find out a few years later that the disastrous concentration of wealth still exists. Oxfam Novib's well-intentioned proposals are, in fact, even a danger, because these plans may put sand in the eyes of those with few assets.

The crux is that we can only solve wealth concentration if we start seriously taxing the absolute value of property or wealth itself as a unit with percentages of 30% or more, with the aim of reducing the wealth of the extremely rich (now up to 200 billion euros) to a healthier level of about 10 million euros. Whether the amount should be exactly 10 million euros, we shall need to investigate further. It may be better to introduce a transition phase and start with a higher amount. It should be about a revolutionary introduction of wealth tax, and not about 'income from wealth tax', or capital income tax, which they want to keep us busy with for another while.

This book is a call for all people to wake up. We should not be lulled to sleep with proposals that do not go far enough! There will really have to be much more pressure to put a ceiling on individual's wealth and redistribute money worldwide. The pressure will have to come from ordinary people, after which politics can take over.

Only then will revolutionary changes come about. Now is the time! The time to make ordinary people aware that they are poor because the rich are so wealthy!

Our unhealthy economies, bankrupt governments, extreme inequalities and the gigantic climate problems we can only solve if we make a revolutionary change, by introducing a Super Rich Tax.

Chapter 3

Five types of people

All money ultimately ends up with the exorbitantly rich

Something is going badly wrong in our world. Inequality, poverty, energy crisis, climate problems and expensive solutions, nitrogen problems, environmental pollution and plastic issues, plus faltering health care and unequal opportunities for children... you name it. There's something wrong with everything, we feel. We seem to have lost our grip on our basic provisions.

Something has to be done. Something revolutionary. Changes must be set in motion, otherwise hard times are going to come for an increasing proportion of the people of our earth.

The great inequality in our societies today has created different types of people, who perceive and experience the world in different ways.

Because I want to explain the necessity of the Super Rich Tax to ALL people, I take into account as much as possible different viewpoints. Therefore, for the purpose of explaining the Super Rich Tax, I recognise the following groups of people, each with their own perspective.

---

1 **The Underprivileged:** people who can barely make ends meet, who have occasional, regular or constant financial concerns and have only the prospect of an underpaid job as their next step. Underprivileged people cannot accumulate wealth, nor do they have the prospect of a better future, one in which they will have a well-paying job. They don't have the bargaining power for this.

---

2 **The Privileged:** people who have the prospect of a well-paying job, and a bargaining power for this. They can make ends meet and can spend money on extra luxuries. They also have the prospect of wealth for the purpose of retirement; approximately between two and four tons of euros.

---

3 **The Rich:** people with assets between 0.4 and 10 million euros.

---

4 **The Extreme Rich:** people with wealth between 10 and 50 million euros.

---

5 **The Exorbitantly Rich:** people with wealth between 0.05 and 200 billion euros.

In total, the world population is now 8 billion people. Below is an estimate of the total number of people in the various categories.

---

1   **The Underprivileged:** 60% of all people, or 4,800,000,000 people are underprivileged.

---

2   **The Privileged:** 35% of all people, or 2,800,000,000 people are privileged.

---

3   **The Rich:** 4.5% of all people, or 360,000,000 people are rich.

---

4   **The Extreme Rich:** 0.4% of all people, or 32,000,000 people are extremely rich.

---

5   **The Exorbitantly Rich:** 0.1% of all people, or 8,000,000 people are exorbitantly rich.

The above percentages are 'approximate' percentages, they have been estimated as accurately as possible by me, and it is possible that they will differ slightly from actual percentages. The big picture remains, and that is the most important, which is that more than half of the total amount of the entire world's money is in the hands of a very small group of exorbitantly rich people.

Did you know that those 0.1% exorbitantly rich collectively hold more than 50% of all the world's money?

'If we don't change the world in a revolutionary way, the 0.1% exorbitantly rich will soon own just 50% but

more than 80%! In other words, almost all the money out there... with all the terrible consequences.'

On www.superrichtax.com you can watch a number of videos explaining this in minute detail.

In the following chapters, I shall explain why you should vote in favour of the Super Rich Tax. It is important for everyone to be sufficiently informed about the consequences of the super-wealth of the group of exorbitantly rich people in the world. Read, talk about it with others, ponder about it and then speak out. You can do so anonymously on www.superrichtax.com.

Chapter 4

The Underprivileged

People who can barely make ends meet

This chapter is written specifically for the underprivileged. Certainly not to pigeonhole these people, because we've already seen that the majority of people on the planet belong to this category. So please don't feel alone.

So, the underprivileged. Underprivileged people include those who cannot or who can barely make ends meet and those who only have the prospect of a low-paying job that will never allow them to accumulate wealth.

An underprivileged person has no chance of getting a better-paying job; they have no bargaining power for this. They should already be happy with their poorly paid job and settle for the salary offered to them. An underprivileged person is almost never in a position to negotiate their salary with their boss.

'Unfortunately, the underprivileged are not the exception. The group of underprivileged people is enormous. About 60% of the world's population is underprivileged, 60% of all people in the entire world live in the same, hopeless situation.'

'Because the large group of underprivileged people have no bargaining power, they are often underpaid. And because they are underpaid, the rich are able to profit again.'

An underprivileged person has no bargaining power in life. But since the underprivileged are part of by far the largest group of the five groups of people in the world, all the underprivileged people combined are able to form a strong group! All the votes of the underprivileged together can make the difference for the introduction of a tax for the super rich: the Super Rich Tax. Because the underprivileged are such a big group, together they form a healthy support base for change!

If the Super Rich Tax is introduced, all the money will no longer remain with the extremely rich and exorbitantly wealthy. The money will then go back into the economy, returning to the underprivileged.

The wealth of the extremely rich and the exorbitantly rich is in the shares of successful companies employing underprivileged and privileged people like you and me. Suppose the company you work for has a thousand employees and it is owned by two people: the shareholders or entrepreneurs. Then a thousand staff together allow those two people at the top to make money. All those staff together create the money for these two shareholders or entrepreneurs. The fact that someone earns something from their own business or from their investment is normal, they are perfectly welcome to, but when they earn more than 10 million from it, it's bad for the economy, as explained in Chapter 2. Indeed, too much ownership by one person makes the economy unhealthier, because it reduces the total amount of available money in the world that can be used as a means of exchange (the actual economy). This causes there to be a small group of exorbitantly rich, as well as an enormously large group of underprivileged people in the world.

We really shouldn't tolerate this anymore. We should – anonymously – vote for the Super Rich Tax. Talk about it with colleagues, friends and family members, read this book, check out www.superrichtax.com and vote!

Because the underprivileged will be able to earn more as a result of this Super Rich Tax, our economies can become healthier. This will also make our governments healthier. It goes like this: the government will be able to acquire higher revenue from the taxes it levies on ordinary people's wages, precisely because those ordinary people earn more! Governments will then grow healthier again, allowing them to introduce more and better initiatives to help everyone find normal paid work. And as our economies become healthier again, there will also be more opportunities for well-paying jobs.

To conclude

Currently money flows from the people with few assets to the rich. This has disastrous consequences, such as even more underprivileged people, and more bankrupt governments and economies.

By taxing the super-rich by means of the Super Rich Tax, money will flow back to ordinary people, restoring healthy economies and governments. As a result, the underprivileged can once again become more advantaged.

Similar to the French Revolution, it is now time for another upheaval: the global Super Rich Tax revolution that we can only initiate by all working together. After all, revolutions are never initiated by the extremely rich, existing rulers or political parties. Revolutions are only initiated from below: by ordinary people.

We don't even have to go on the streets and cause upheaval (like in the French Revolution) anymore. All you have to do is vote en masse on superrichtax.com and the revolutionary ball will start rolling. Billions of votes cannot be ignored by the current political parties and those in power. Individually, as an underprivileged person, you have no bargaining power, but as the largest group on the planet (4.8 billion people!), you have very strong bargaining power. So it is time for everyone, including the underprivileged, to unite and vote en masse for the Super Rich Tax.

Chapter 5

The Privileged
People who can make ends meet

In this chapter, you will read about the privileged. The people with prospects of a good-paying job, who have bargaining power, who can make a good living and spend money on extra luxuries, and who also have the prospect of wealth for the purpose of retirement (approximately between 2 and 4 tons of euros).

You are lucky, you are among the 35% of the world's population who can live a happy life. You are able to feel good about yourself because of the luxuries you can afford, such as far-away holidays, a nice car and a comfy home.
Because you can choose from different jobs, you have bargaining power, which means you are probably paid well.

As a result, you manage to build up wealth for retirement, between approx. 2 and 4 tons of euros. What you may not realise, however, is that many economies and governments are in increasingly bad shape, making it questionable whether your children and grandchildren will also have similar privileges. Since you are part of quite a large group that exist in today's world, your vote can make a significant difference and create a healthy support base for the introduction of the Super Rich Tax.

When the Super Rich Tax is introduced, the money will no longer remain with the rich, but instead our economies will become healthy again thanks to amount of money that will be available for use as a medium of exchange. And with healthier economies, the underprivileged are more likely to get better-paying jobs. Allowing your children and grandchildren to also live happy, opportunity-filled lives.

The wealth of the extremely rich and the exorbitantly wealthy lies mainly in the shares of successful companies, whom the underprivileged and privileged work for. Suppose the company you work for consists of a thousand employees. The company is owned by two shareholders. In the current situation, these thousand employees ensure the two shareholders make a lot of money. All employees combined create a lot of capital for the two shareholders. As explained in Chapter 2, it is normal for an entrepreneur to make money from their business, but when we speak of amounts of over 10 million euros, this is bad for the economy. Indeed, too much ownership by one person makes the economy unhealthier, because the total amount of available money used as a medium of exchange (the actual economy) then decreases. Precisely this is the reason why there is currently a small group of extremely rich and exorbitantly rich people in the world.

We really shouldn't tolerate this anymore. We should – anonymously – vote for the Super Rich Tax. Talk about it with colleagues, friends and family members, read this book, check out www.superrichtax.com and vote!

Because the underprivileged will earn more with the introduction of the Super Rich Tax, our economies will also be healthier. The taxes flowing from ordinary people to governments will increase, putting more money in the state coffers. Once those governments are healthy again, they can implement more and better initiatives to help everyone get well-paying jobs. No to mention, as our economies become healthier again, there will also be more opportunities in terms of jobs.

To conclude

Currently money flows from ordinary people to the rich, with disastrous consequences such as an even greater number of underprivileged people and more bankrupt governments and economies. By means of the Super Rich Tax, the money will flow back to ordinary people, allowing healthy economies and governments to emerge again. As a result, the underprivileged can become more advantaged again, and growth for all becomes possible. It also increases the chances that your own children and grandchildren can lead lives as happy as yours.

Similar to the French Revolution, it is now time for another upheaval: the global Super Rich Tax revolution that we can only initiate by all working together. After all, revolutions are never initiated by the extremely rich, existing rulers or political parties, they are only initiated from below: by ordinary people.

We don't even have to go on the streets and cause upheaval (like in the French Revolution) anymore. All you have to do is vote en masse (anonymously) on www.superrichtax.com and the revolutionary ball will start rolling. Billions of votes really cannot be ignored by the current political parties and those in power.

Individually, as a privileged person, you have no political influence, but together you form a large group, allowing you to have a voice! It is time for the privileged to unite and vote en masse for the Super Rich Tax.

Chapter 6

The Rich
Between 0.4 and 10 million euros

This chapter was written for the rich. People with assets between 0.4 and 10 million euros. People who can live quite autonomously thanks to their assets. For example, they no longer have to work. If they do, they only do it because they enjoy to do so. In this way they have bargaining power. These are people who can easily make ends meet and spend money on many extra luxuries.

You are very lucky, you are among the 4.5% of the world's population who can live a very happy life. You built your wealth with a successful business, or you have an extremely well-paying job with an excellent bonus plan, or you acquired your wealth through inheritance.

You feel good about yourself thanks to the luxuries you can afford because you worked hard - or your father or grandfather did - and you've managed to avoid the risks of bankruptcy.

Because you have a good reserve – or assets – you can be quite autonomous in choosing an occupation.

You may even not have to work, but it's still nice if some money is preserved for your children and grandchildren as well. Because you can choose from several well-paying jobs and you can seek jobs in an autonomous way, you have a very good bargaining position. With your income and perhaps the extra money you earn from your property, you can increase your wealth even further.

You seem to be doing well, but what you don't realise is that it's going to be very difficult to pass on your wealth to your children and grandchildren. After all, compared to the extremely rich and the exorbitantly rich, you are – relatively – not that rich at all. The extremely rich have up to 50 times as much wealth as you, and the exorbitantly rich may even have up to 20,000 times as much wealth. In the stock markets, you are hopeless against these giants in terms of bargaining power in the longer term. The extremely rich and exorbitantly rich will acquire your shares in successful companies in the long run. Your children and grandchildren will most likely rejoin the group of ordinary people, and thus depend on income from a job.

What you may also not realise is that economies and governments are increasingly worse off, making it questionable whether your children and grandchildren will be able to live as fortunate a life as you do.

If you don't believe that you (and your children) are losing wealth to the extremely rich and the exorbitantly rich in the long term, I recommend you watch Professor Jan Tobochnik's video. The video can be found on www.superrichtax.com. In this video, Tobochnik explains how a process of wealth concentration is taking place in the world today, after which there will only one person remain with all the money in the world.

When the Super Rich Tax is introduced, your wealth up to and including 10 million will at least be secured. Your wealth can therefore no longer be taken over from a worse negotiating position in the long term by the extremely rich and exorbitantly rich. Economies and governments will also become healthy again, so that your children and grandchildren have the opportunity for a happy, promising life.

It feels intolerable, right? That you will soon lose your wealth to the extremely rich and exorbitantly rich? I recommend you share this Super Rich Tax book, watch the videos on www.superrichtax.com, talk about it with colleagues, friends or family members and then vote (completely anonymously) for the Super Rich Tax.

To conclude

Currently money is flowing from the common people to the rich, with disastrous consequences, such as an even greater number of disadvantaged people and more bankrupt governments and economies. With the Super Rich Tax money will flow back to ordinary people, allowing healthy economies and governments to emerge again. This allows the underprivileged to become more privileged again, and growth for all becomes possible. It also increases your chances that your own children and grandchildren will lead lives as happy as yours.

Similar to the French Revolution, it is now time for another upheaval: the global Super Rich Tax revolution that we can only initiate by all working together. After all, revolutions are never initiated by the extremely rich, existing rulers or political parties, revolutions are only initiated from below: by ordinary people.

We don't even have to go on the streets and cause upheaval (like in the French Revolution) anymore. All you have to do is vote (anonymously) on www.superrichtax.com and the revolutionary ball will start rolling.

Chapter 7

The Extremely Rich

Between 10 and 50 million euros

This chapter is written for the extremely rich. People with assets between 10 and 50 million euros. People whose extreme wealth allows them to be autonomous and therefore not have to work, or do work on their own terms - work they enjoy. The extremely rich have excellent bargaining power, they can easily make ends meet and they can spend a lot of money on extreme luxuries.

You are very lucky, you are among the very limited 0.4% of the world's population that can live an extremely happy life. You have accumulated wealth with a successful business, or you have an extremely well-paying job with an excellent bonus plan, or you obtained your wealth through inheritance.

You probably feel good about yourself, you or your parents or grandparents worked very hard and also took many risks for the extreme luxury you can afford. Because you have healthy reserves, or assets, you can be autonomous in making choices throughout your life. Maybe you're still working, but not necessarily.

You make sure your millions of dollars are preserved for your children and preferably even your grandchildren. Because you can live fairly autonomous thanks to your assets, you have a very good bargaining position. This allows you to organise your own life, maybe even work, to your liking. If you can make extra money through that work in addition to the money you earn from your assets, you will increase your wealth even further. All for your children and grandchildren.

What you don't yet realise is that it's going to be very difficult to pass on all your family wealth to your children and grandchildren. After all, relative to the exorbitantly rich, you are not that rich at all. The exorbitantly rich are far more wealthy than you. In stock markets, in terms of bargaining power, you are hopeless against these giants in the long run. Indeed, the exorbitantly rich will buy your shares in successful companies from you in the long run. As a result, your children and grandchildren will very likely go back to being ordinary people, and depend on the income from their jobs again. What you may also not realise is, that economies and governments are increasingly worse off, making it questionable whether your children and grandchildren will be able to live such a life of opportunity as you do.

If you don't believe that you (or your children) will soon be losing quite a lot of wealth to the exorbitantly rich, I recommend you watch Professor Jan Tobochnik's video on www.superrichtax.com. In this video, Tobochnik explains that there is a process of wealth concentration going on in the world where eventually only one person in the world will remain who will own all the world's money.

Once the Super Rich Tax has been introduced, your wealth will be secured up to at least 10 million euros. This 10 million euros won't, from a worse bargaining position, be able to be acquired by the exorbitantly rich. With the Super Rich Tax system, economies and governments will become healthy again, increasing the chances that your children and grandchildren too can live a happy life.

That you will soon lose your wealth to the exorbitantly rich is intolerable. I encourage you to discuss this book with colleagues, friends and family members, and check out the Super Rich Tax website. Chances are you too will vote (anonymously) on www.superrichtax.com.

To conclude

Currently money flows from the non-rich to the rich, with disastrous consequences such as more bankrupt governments and economies and even more underprivileged people who, working 40 hours a week or more, still have too little income to make ends meet. With the Super Rich Tax, money will flow back to ordinary people, restoring healthy economies and governments. As a result, the chance of a happy life for your children and grandchildren increases significantly.

After the French revolution it is time for a new upheaval: the global Super Rich Tax revolution that the non-rich are going to initiate. After all, revolutions are never initiated by the rich, existing rulers or political parties, revolutions are initiated from below: by ordinary people.

Take a look on www.superrichtax.com and read how the non-rich are going to unite and vote en masse for the Super Rich Tax.

Chapter 8

The Exorbitantly Rich

Between 0.05 and 200 billion euros

This chapter is written especially for the exorbitantly rich. People with wealth between 50 million and 200 billion euros. People whose exorbitant wealth gives them complete autonomy and makes them feel untouchable.

A few exorbitantly rich people think they can single-handedly save the world and humanity by spending millions of euros, setting up projects, donating money to science, all as a form of charity. Sometimes we see a bit of megalomania in this, which isn't surprising. With such a huge fortune, you belong to an exclusive club, and your world view is simply different from that of someone who has to work six days a week in the catering industry and struggles to pay their rent, electricity bill, property tax, water treatment tax, health insurance premium and whatnot.

Indeed, ordinary people often cannot even put a decent meal on the table seven days a week anymore.

It is not at all strange that some of you, with your assets, moving into your own little club, are gradually getting an unrealistic worldview. It's also not surprising that a few of you might get a few narcissistic traits or become addicted to the risks you can take. Mass psychologist Jaap van Ginneken has done research on exorbitantly rich. This research has shown that people who spend a very long time at the summit, perhaps for generations, can suffer from altitude sickness. Figurative height then, the study refers to it as 'psychologically disturbed'.

You are very lucky, you belong to the rare 0.1% of the world's population that can live an exorbitant, disproportionate life. You have built your wealth with a successful business and expanded it further by buying shares of other highly successful companies, or you have inherited this wealth, or quite possibly obtained it illegally through political abuse of power.

You feel good about yourself because you have taken some well-considered risks in life. You forced your luck, you occasionally say. There is a chance, though, that some of you have become a little different because of that enormous wealth and all those successes. Maybe some of you have caught a little of that altitude sickness, which makes that voice inside say that it's perfectly normal for you to have so much power. You think you have achieved it all by yourself, and you believe you pay way too much tax. That is the reason why you live in Monaco, or whatever tax haven your wealth manager advised. You are very grateful to him, because actually, relatively speaking, you don't pay that much tax at all. It is a normal psychological process that surely a fair number of exorbitantly wealthy people go through, as mass psychologist Jaap van Ginneken explains.

What you don't realise is that the world's economies and governments are in increasingly worse shape due to the presence of exorbitant wealth, leaving the question of how the world, humanity and your children will fare in the long run.

To conclude

Currently all the world's money flows to an extremely small group of exorbitantly rich people, with disastrous consequences such as even more underprivileged people and more bankrupt governments and economies. With the Super Rich Tax, the money will flow back to ordinary people, allowing healthy economies and governments to re-establish themselves, and as a result, the underprivileged can once again become more advantaged.

The French revolution was nothing compared to this new upheaval; the global Super Rich Tax revolution that the underprivileged are about to initiate. After all, revolutions are never initiated by the extremely rich, existing rulers or political parties, revolutions are only initiated from below: by ordinary people.

Soon after the Super Rich Tax is implemented, the economies and governments will become healthy again. You – and your exorbitantly wealthy colleagues – are at the forefront of saving the world, humanity, and your children.

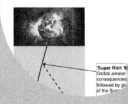

Chapter 9

How the concentration of wealth came about

Extreme inequality did not emerge until four thousand years ago

No extreme inequality for three million years

For three million years, all the humanoids from which we evolved lived as itinerant hunter-gatherers in groups of about eighty individuals. These humanoids were true generalists. Each group had a chief, who was the wisest (from a holistic point of view) to make the best decisions for his tribe. These tribal leaders usually had a slightly larger hut or tent and perhaps got slightly better food than the rest of the tribesmen, but these differences, besides being minimal, were as obvious to everyone as they were functional. In fact, this low level of property differences and hierarchy created peace and stability in the group. There was a fair, or reasonable, distribution of all wealth. For three million years, there was no extreme inequality in the world.

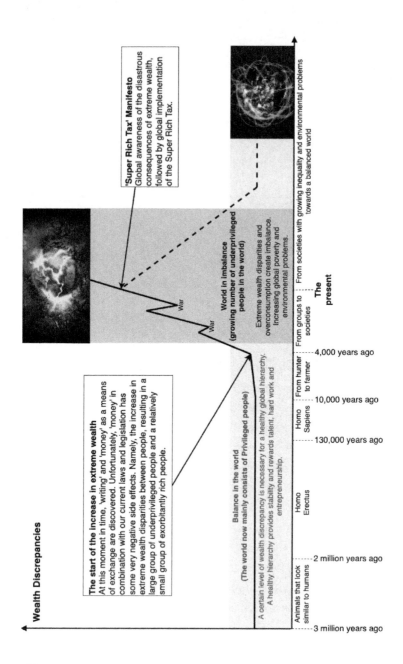

Wealth Discrepancies

The start of the increase in extreme wealth
At this moment in time, 'writing' and 'money' as a means of exchange are discovered. Unfortunately, 'money' in combination with our current laws and legislation has some very negative side effects. Namely, the increase in extreme wealth disparities between people, resulting in a large group of underprivileged people and a relatively small group of exorbitantly rich people.

'Super Rich Tax' Manifesto
Global awareness of the disastrous consequences of extreme wealth, followed by global implementation of the Super Rich Tax.

World in imbalance (growing number of underprivileged people in the world)

Extreme wealth disparities and overconsumption create imbalance. Increasing global poverty and environmental problems.

War

War

Balance in the world
(The world now mainly consists of Privileged people)

A certain level of wealth discrepancy is necessary for a healthy global hierarchy. A healthy hierarchy provides stability and rewards talent, hard work and entrepreneurship.

From societies with growing inequality and environmental problems towards a balanced world

The present

From groups to societies

From hunter to farmer

Homo Sapiens

Homo Erectus

Animals that look similar to humans

----- 3 million years ago
----- 2 million years ago
----- 130,000 years ago
----- 10,000 years ago
----- 4,000 years ago

Extreme inequality only came about four thousand years ago

About ten thousand to four thousand years ago, people slowly transformed from wandering hunter/gatherers in groups to landowners and farmers. When the phenomenon of 'trade', and later the phenomena of 'money' and 'credit' emerged, extreme inequality was around the corner.

The tax system was responsible for the rest. Land ownership, money, credit and taxes are the causes of today's extreme inequality in the world. After all, money can be used not only as a medium of exchange, but also as a means of storage or possession. The discovery of money suddenly made it possible for man to hoard money indefinitely, as a form of possession.

In itself, possession or wealth is not a bad thing, were it not for the fact that a person with an extreme amount of possession or wealth can acquire a position of power that is far too great, and can then control those with less possession or wealth. The tribal elder is no longer the 'wisest' man in the group, instead it is the richest.

One negative side effect of money as a store of value is that it unfairly improves one's bargaining position. As a result, one can more easily make advantageous and better business deals than people with less money. Because of this unfair mechanism, money has been flowing from the underprivileged to the super-rich for some four thousand years.

This process of concentration of wealth has meant that more than half of the world's total money is now in the hands of the 0.1% richest.

Eight billion people in the world currently have less money than the world's 0.1% richest.

As human social structures have become increasingly complex (from tribes consisting of about eighty people to cities where tens of millions live together) and as we have changed from generalists to specialists, there are no longer tribal elders with a holistic view. Due to the complexity of today's world with all its specialties and intricate social structures, we have become inhibited, and are unable to see the absurdity of the current situation.

Thus, we no longer realise that the people with the most money pay relatively the least amount of taxes, and thus contribute relatively little to the community.

The wealth of millionaires and billionaires is taxed minimally, even though these people have to work zero hours for it.
Rich people simply need to acquire property and rent it out, or hire an advisor to make smart investments. To kill time, rich people frequently go on vacation, or they do charity work.

In addition to having a better bargaining position, there are also rules of the game that greatly favour the rich and super-rich. As a result, money has been flowing from ordinary people to those rich and super-rich for four thousand years. In a healthy world, this money would flow the other way around. Capital would flow from the super-rich to ordinary people, and certainly not the other way around, as is the case now.

Ordinary people are the basis for a healthy economy. A group that is just slightly richer than it is now, will make even the government richer. A richer government offers more opportunities to restore privilege to the underprivileged. Our current path can only be fixed with the introduction of a global Super Rich Tax.

Only then can we get the money flowing in the right direction again. For more information, take a look at the inequality chart as included in this chapter, and watch the videos on www.superrichtax.com. Vote for the Super Rich Tax anonymously via the 'I support the Super Rich Tax' button!

We'll finally be able to move the planet in the right direction again.

Chapter 10

We've discovered that extreme power should be taxed

The new basic story of humanity

Help poverty reduction and environmental protection with the new basic story of humanity!

There are two versions of reality in our world:

---

1 The physical reality, which one can perceive with their senses. The reality one can see, hear, smell, taste and feel. For example, one sees a house, hears a storm, smells perfume, tastes an apple and feels sandpaper. A physical reality can be created by nature or by humans, although humans are of course also part of nature.

---

2 The narrative reality we create as humanity by telling each other stories. For example, consider a national border, a company, religions or national laws. I especially recommend Harari's book Sapiens, for a more detailed explanation of narrative reality.

As humans, we tell each other stories, and this allows us to work together in much larger groups than animals do. The unifying factor of the group is no longer the family or the location, but the story the whole group believes in. For example, most people in our world attach great importance to countries' borders. When one no longer believes in the integrity of national borders, wars may start, such as the one Russia initiated in 2022.

Another example of a narrative reality is a company. A company only exists by the grace of the stories people tell each other. Companies are not located around every corner, in fact they're often based in another country or continent. You don't witness them with your own eyes, and yet you have an impression of them. So while you cannot see, hear, smell, taste or touch a company, you have a certain sense about it. Once someone starts a business, it will have a name and will be registered somewhere. From this moment, we can say that the company 'exists' and we do everything we can to tell stories about that company. Harari explains this very clearly in his book Sapiens. I can highly recommend giving this book a read.

If a certain group believes in a certain story, then that group will behave according to that story. A story incites certain behaviours within a group. This group behaviour creates a new physical reality.

A new physical reality can emerge from shared stories. Take for example the story of Sinterklaas, a Dutch children's festival about a man who, together with his helpers, called 'Black Petes', hands out presents to children. A few years ago, most Dutch people were still enjoying this festival that has been celebrated for almost a century. Until the moment that more and more people became aware of the fact that using make-up to blacken your pale, white Dutch face to play Sinterklaas's helper is not OK, and besides: that it is neither OK to let black-skinned people play a white man's helper. And, although intended amusedly, they are also portrayed as being a bit of silly and clumsy helpers...

Over recent years, the story of Sinterklaas has been updated. The story has changed, it has grown with the times. For example, Sinterklaas's helpers are now called 'Soot-swept Petes', they are no longer painted black and the new Petes are smart. Sinterklaas and those celebrating no longer need to be considered racist. The new story has positively changed reality. No more people are unintentionally hurt by the Sinterklaas festivities.

By this I want to make it clear that the stories we believe in, age-old stories and new stories, have a great impact on the physical reality we experience every day, that is, the reality we see, hear, smell, taste or feel. Some stories affect physical reality more than others. Some stories are told only locally, and then apply to that region. Now I would like to talk about the stories that have a great impact on all of us. On all people throughout the world. Stories alongside those of our religions, alongside the stories of our countries of origin. I want to talk about the stories that have even more impact on us, and those are: laws. Interestingly, while the core of these 'stories' are often similar in many different countries, they can also show variation.

There is one story that is even more impactful than the high-impact stories I just mentioned. And that is the so-called basic story of all humanity. The story of all of us. Because we all believe in this basic story, even more than any other, it has by far the biggest impact on the current, physical reality of our planet. What is this basic story of humanity that we all believe in right now?

About four thousand years ago, we told each other a story about coins that could be used as a medium of exchange. Curious as we were – and still are – we began to use and collect those coins. Then we told each other a story about how it might be helpful if there were to be a 'government' that would regulate and pay for the common facilities for our group. All of us, no one excepted, would contribute a coin to that every year. This gave the 'government' the means to do and create the things that were useful to all of us.

Building dikes to protect us from water, providing clean drinking water, building roads, and later also maintaining things like street lights, a fire department, a field watchman, as well as sending mail, not to mention offering education. It all cost us more and more coins over time, but we gladly gave them up.

This is the basic story of humanity that we have believed in for four thousand years now. So far, there seems to be nothing wrong with this basic story. Yet it appears to have a nasty side effect. This basic story where we have been for a long time, and still to this day, and which all of us believe in, creates a gigantic concentration of wealth among a handful of exorbitantly wealthy people. At the same time, this basic story unfortunately ensures that the already large group of underprivileged people in the world is ever increasing. So that means that all the money in the world is distributed among fewer and fewer people. If we don't adapt this time-honoured basic story of humanity to the present day very soon, our economies will become increasingly unhealthy, our governments increasingly poor, and then the already large group of underprivileged will become much larger. Indeed, if we do not start adapting this so-called basic story of humanity to modern times very soon, it does not look good for overall humanity.

But now the good news!

Fortunately, the basic story of humanity is adaptable. Pretty easily even. This way we can avoid the disastrous consequences of the basic story. As humanity, we can believe in the new basic story, in which we tax not only income but also extreme wealth. That way, we stop the flow of money flowing towards the super-rich, and all the money in the world becomes better distributed. More people will get opportunities, instead of - as is the case now - fewer and fewer people.

In brief

Because we all believe in the current basic story of humanity, all the money in the world is now distributed among increasingly fewer people, namely among the group of super-rich. With all its disastrous consequences. If we all start believing in humanity's new basic story, all the world's money will be distributed to regular people again, instead of just the super-rich. This will create healthy economies and governments worldwide, so that we can reduce poverty, allowing us to structurally solve climate and environmental problems.

Let it be known anonymously that you too believe in this new grassroots story! Vote anonymously on www.superrichtax.com.

Vote and spread the word!

Chapter 11

The six phases
People are becoming increasingly aware of the disastrous effects of extreme wealth

First phase

In the first phase, the first group of people in the world becomes aware of the disastrous effects of extreme wealth.

Second phase

In the second phase, more and more people understand that extreme wealth is the world's core problem, and the number of people anonymously voting for the Super Rich Tax at www.superrichtax.com grows. On the 'Votes by Country' page, anyone can see how many people have already voted for the plan - anonymously and by country.

Third phase

In the third phase, political parties in certain countries are actually beginning to gain support for the Super Rich Tax in their campaigns. The Super Rich Tax becomes an increasingly well-known concept around the world, and support is emerging in more and more countries, both on the streets, in villages and towns, and in politics.

Fourth phase

In the fourth stage, a number of governments of major economies together conclude that the number of supportive countries is sufficiently large to implement the Super Rich Tax jointly.

Fifth phase

In the fifth phase, the remaining countries will also introduce the Super Rich Tax to create a healthy and balanced economy and government.

Sixth phase

In the sixth stage (the final stage), the effects of the Super Rich Tax manifest themselves, and healthy economies and governments emerge, so that we can finally structurally solve world problems such as poverty and environmental pollution.

Chapter 12

Frequently Asked Questions
And their answers!

Who came up with the unhealthy rule of taxing only income and not extreme wealth?

As humanity, we invented this rule ourselves. We tax only income, not extreme wealth. As a result, we now have a small group of extremely wealthy people on our planet, which will have disastrous consequences for people and nature. These extremely rich suck all the money away from us, the ordinary people. Because the health of our economies is mainly determined by our situation, there are now many unhealthy economies that we try to keep afloat by all sorts of means and measures. Current governments have accumulated an ever-increasing mountain of debt because they are largely paid for by the tax-paying, but thus increasingly poor, ordinary people.

And now the good news!

We can easily extend the current game rule and start taxing extreme wealth as well, so that healthy economies and governments are created almost by themselves. It is actually quite simple: all the money in the world should circulate among as large a group of people as possible to have a healthy economy, rather than among as small a group as possible, as is the case now. Because all the world's money now circulates among an ever-smaller group of people, there are now all unhealthy economies and governments that have to be kept alive with all sorts of artificial measures. By means of the Super Rich Tax, all the world's money will circulate among an ever-increasing pool of people, restoring sanity to our economies and governments and allowing us to finally, structurally solve poverty and environmental degradation.

What does casting my anonymous vote mean? What about implementation of the actual plans? Isn't this an exercise in futility?

A country can introduce the Super Rich Tax only if the super-rich cannot easily move or divert their wealth to the countries that have not yet introduced the Super Rich Tax. To avoid economic disadvantages for the first countries to introduce this tax, it is a good idea to create global support in advance. If that support becomes apparent, by publishing the number of people which voted anonymously, several large countries can start implementing this Super Rich Tax at the same time, without the super rich being able to quickly move their money to a country that has not yet introduced this tax. For that reason, the website includes a counter with the number of (anonymous) votes per country, which acts as an indication of support.

So by means of this manifesto, we can create measurable support for political parties around the world to include the Super Rich Tax in their campaigns.
After all, political parties can only do so if they can increase their existing number of seats, or have a better chance of getting elected.

The fact that something is difficult should not be a reason not to take the first step. As Harari states in his book Sapiens, 'If enough people believe in a new story, the story becomes a new reality'.

Is it good if governments get richer? After all, governments are not always efficient and, in poor countries, often even corrupt.
The introduction of the Super Rich Tax is not intended to bail out governments. Indeed, the main consequence of the Super Rich Tax is for the super rich to divide some of their wealth above 10 million euros among their own employees. The super-rich will be more positive about this approach than paying taxes to their government. In the long run, the Super Rich Tax's new rules of the game will create a new, much fairer distribution of wealth that benefits everyone economically.

Won't the super-rich move their wealth to the countries that do not apply this tax?
Yes, that is certainly a risk. Therefore, this Super Rich Tax can only be introduced if the world's major countries (economies) work together and introduce it simultaneously. This is the reason

why we add up all the anonymous votes for this manifesto by country. This will allow each government to see where they stand, in terms of the rankings. (See the 'Votes by Country' item in the main menu on www.superrichtax.com).

Opponents sometimes refer to the Super Rich Tax as the 'Envy Tax'. Is this jealousy?

I'm sure it's not jealousy. Most ordinary people enjoy the life they lead. Me too. I am convinced, however, that if we don't change anything now, more and more ordinary people, both the underprivileged and the privileged, and probably also the rich and maybe even the extremely rich, will start living unhappy lives because the current system only makes the group of exorbitantly rich ever richer, at the expense of other people.

Why is this wealth tax an emotional issue for many people?

Because the basic rules of today's world are being changed. A new story will emerge. This means people have to say goodbye to the old. And you know: change is always difficult, for everyone. It always takes a while before we are willing to let go of the old and step into something new. Because many people prefer to leave things as they are, emotions sometimes run high. Especially among the exorbitantly rich! We will have to understand this, and will try to maintain an understanding between as many people as possible.

What happens next? What action do we take?

We are currently in the first phase of the Super Rich Tax, as described in the last chapter of the manifesto (version 1.0, February 2023). In this phase, the first people will become aware of the destructive effects of the extreme wealth of a small group of people who own half the world's money. The first people who become aware of this will vote for this manifesto. To grow the number of voices worldwide, we will:

---

1 promote this manifesto through the Internet, social media, TV and newspapers,

---

2 recruit sponsors to expand the website to multiple countries/ languages, and set up Facebook campaigns worldwide,

---

3 find famous people and influencers willing to further promote the manifesto, and

---

4 find volunteers who want to help with all of the above.

For information on the other phases, please refer to the respective chapter in this book.

There are currently already initiatives by the super-rich themselves to do something about wealth tax. Doesn't this mean we're moving in the right direction already?
Indeed, there are noises from a few super-rich people indicating that they are quite willing to pay a little wealth tax, but these proposals do not go nearly far enough. In fact, these suggestions may even be a danger, because they can throw sand in the eyes of those with little wealth. These proposals of a few well-meaning super-rich people do not go nearly far enough. For example, they come up with proposals for paying 2 to 5% wealth tax. These percentages are not going to stop the disastrous concentration of

wealth on our planet. In Chapter 2, I explain why these rates are not enough and only have a dampening effect on the growth of wealth concentration. In other words, wealth concentration will continue to increase, only slightly less harshly, but unfortunately just as destructively. In fact, the danger is that these friendly proposals from the super-rich will lull ordinary people with few assets to sleep.

This book is a call for all people to wake up. We will not be lulled to sleep by the proposal of the super-rich to start paying a tiny bit of wealth tax. Never mind that we should praise the super-rich who come up with these proposals: they really do have good intentions after all!

There has to be a considerable pressure from below indicating that it really is high time for a new story. Without that pressure, these meagre, 'good intentions' of the super-rich are not going to get us anywhere at all. The super-rich simply operate within the frameworks of today's world, and then you'll indeed end up with only 2% to 5% wealth tax. But things really need to be different! There needs to be a new basic story, because with this 2% to 5% of wealth tax, you only keep the common people happy for a while, while inequality just keeps growing.

There will really have to be much more pressure to put a ceiling on individual's wealth and redistribute money worldwide. That pressure will have to come from ordinary people, after which politics can take over. Only then will revolutionary changes come about. Remember the French Revolution? Now is exactly the time! The time to make ordinary people aware that they are poor because the rich are so wealthy!

Doesn't the manifesto simplify reality too much?
You may well be right about that. However, we need to make a statement now, so that the outlines become clear. With too much nuance, things often become muddled.

That way, sand has been thrown in our eyes for far too long. If we wish to save humanity, ordinary people around the world must stand up now for what they have a right to: a decent distribution of wealth!

In other words, vote on the website for the introduction of the Super Rich Tax.

Chapter 13

Vote now

Save the underprivileged and all our children

A brief summary of the Super Rich Tax

The Super Rich Tax is actually quite logical and simple.

Working people are the foundation of our economies. As the extremely rich suck all the money away from the working class, today's economies are becoming increasingly unhealthy. We have to use all kinds of measures to keep them afloat.

Working people fund the government. While the extremely rich are sucking all the money out of the working class, governments are taking on more and more debt. Governments themselves have insufficient financial resources to solve the problems. For one coin, they cannot build a bridge.

The solution is truly simple

People are starting to see the downside of extreme wealth and realise that all the money is being sucked out of the working class, bankrupting our economies and governments. If enough people become aware of this and there is sufficient global support for the introduction of the Super Rich Tax, then we can introduce this tax in several countries simultaneously. This way, money does not remain with the super-rich, but flows back to working people. This allows our economies and governments to become healthy again, making it possible to finally solve poverty and environmental pollution in a structural manner.

All current measures to solve poverty and environmental degradation will get a huge boost with the help of the Super Rich Tax. It is a necessary step to change the world for the better.

Vote anonymously now on www.superrichtax.com for implementing the Super Rich Tax and spread the Super Rich Tax manifesto within your network.

Spread the word and save the world!

Bibliography

I have drawn inspiration from the following sources:

Book *De bril van Darwin*, Mark Nelissen. 2000. Publisher:
Lannoo

Book *Sapiens*, Yuval Noah Harari. 2018. Publisher: Thomas Rap

YouTube videos by Thomas Piketty, economist from a historical
and statistical point of view

YouTube video by Peter F. Ricchiuti, clinical Professor of Business
Administration

YouTube video by Jan Tobochnik, professor of Natural Sciences

Article in *HP/De Tijd*. 3 October 2022 De grootste ramp blijkt de
oenige mensheid zelf, Nathalie Huigsloot

Book *Grillig – Klimaat, chaos en publieke opinie*, Jaap van
Ginneken, 2022. Publisher: Mazirel Press